~A BINGO BOOK~

The Law Bingo Book

COMPLETE BINGO GAME IN A BOOK

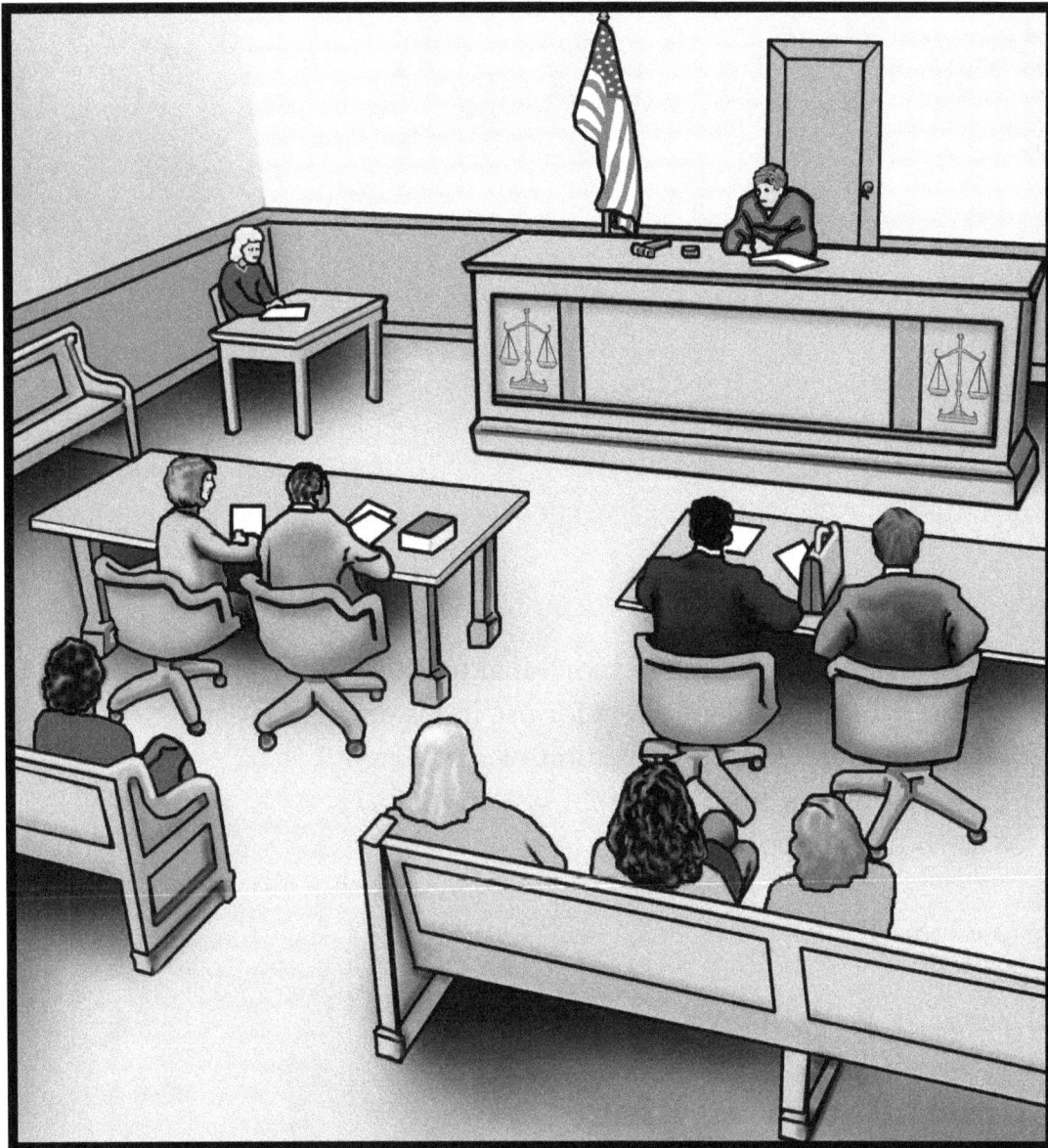

Written By Rebecca Stark

ISBN 978-0-87386-475-6

Educational Books 'n' Bingo

Printed in the U.S.A.

THE LAW BINGO DIRECTIONS

INCLUDED:

List of Terms

Templates for Additional Terms and Clues

2 Clues per Term

30 Unique Bingo Cards

Markers

1. **Either cut apart the book or make copies of ALL the sheets. You might want to make an extra copy of the clue sheets to use for introduction and review. Keep the sheets in an envelope for easy reuse.**

2. Cut apart the call cards with terms and clues.

3. Pass out one bingo card per student. There are enough for a class of 30.

4. Pass out markers. You may cut apart the markers included in this book or use any other small items of your choice.

5. Decide whether or not you will require the entire card to be filled. Requiring the entire card to be filled provides a better review. However, if you have a short time to fill, you may prefer to have them do the just the border or some other format. Tell the class before you begin what is required.

6. There are 50 terms. Read the list before you begin. If there are any terms that have not been covered in class, you may want to read to the students the term and clues before you begin.

7. There is a blank space in the middle of each card. You can instruct the students to use it as a free space or you can write in answers to cover terms not included. Of course, in this case you would create your own clues. (Templates provided.)

8. Shuffle the cards and place them in a pile. Two or three clues are provided for each term. If you plan to play the game with the same group more than once, you might want to choose a different clue for each game. If not, you may choose to use more than one clue.

9. Be sure to keep the cards you have used for the present game in a separate pile. When a student calls, "Bingo," he or she will have to verify that the correct answers are on his or her card AND that the markers were placed in response to the proper questions. Pull out the cards that are on the student's card keeping them in the order they were used in the game. Read each clue as it was given and ask the student to identify the correct answer from his or her card.

10. If the student has the correct answers on the card AND has shown that they were marked in response to the *correct questions,* then that student is the winner and the game is over. If the student does not have the correct answers on the card OR he or she marked the answers in response to *the wrong questions,* then the game continues until there is a proper winner.

11. If you want to play again, reshuffle the cards and begin again.

Have fun!

TERMS

acquit (acquittal)	homicide(s)
alibi	incarceration (incarcerated)
allegation	indictment
appeal	judge(s)
arraignment	judicial
attorney-at-law (attorneys)	jury
bail	law
bailiff	liability (liable)
battery	malice
civil	Miranda rule
closing argument	misdemeanor(s)
contract	motive
court	murder
crime	objection
defendant	plaintiff
defense	plea
deliberation	prosecution
double jeopardy	reasonable doubt
due process	sentence
evidence	testimony
examination	theft
felony (-ies)	trial
forensic	verdict
fraud	warrant
guilty	witness

Additional Terms

Choose as many additional terms as you would like and write them in the squares. Repeat each as desired.
Cut out the squares and randomly distribute them to the class.
Instruct the students to place their square on the center space of their card.

Clues for Additional Terms

Write two clues for each of your additional terms.

1. 2.	1. 2.
1. 2.	1. 2. .
1. 2.	1. 2.

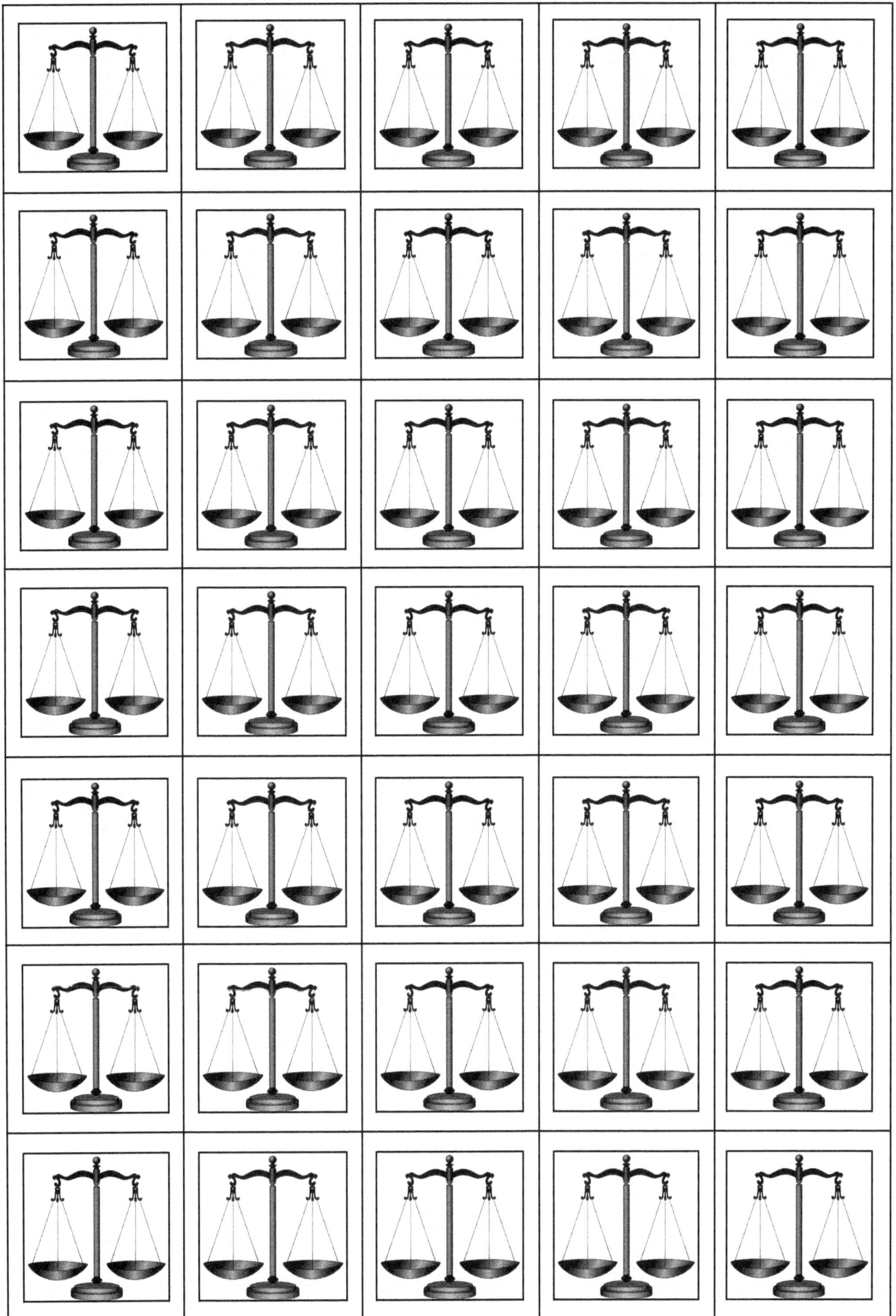

acquit (acquittal) 1. To free someone from a criminal charge by a verdict of not guilty is to ___. 2. To ___ is to "declare not guilty." 3. When a jury finds a verdict of not guilty, the defendant gets an ___.	**alibi** 1. An ___ is a form of defense wherein the accused tries to prove he or she was in some other place when the offense was committed. 2. Opportunity is whether or not the defendant had the chance to commit the crime. It is often disproved by use of an ___. 3. An ___ can prove the accused was not able to commit the crime.
allegation 1. An ___ is a statement of the accusation to be resolved in court. 2. An assertion that someone has done something illegal, especially one made without proof, is an ___. 3. It is a statement of what a party to a legal action will try to prove.	**appeal** 1. To ___ is to apply to a higher court to reverse a decision of a lower court. 2. The Supreme Court is the highest court of ___ in the United States. 3. If a defense attorney believes that the court's decision was not correct, he or she can file for an ___.
arraignment 1. It is the process during which the accused is brought to court, told the charges, and asked to make a plea of guilt or innocence. 2. Complete this analogy: acquit : acquittal :: arraign : ___ 3. During an ___, the accused, now called the defendant, is read the charges and advised of his or her rights.	**attorney-at-law (attorneys)** 1. A synonym for ___ is lawyer, but to be called an ___, one must pass the bar exam and be approved to practice in his or her jurisdiction. 2. An ___ is legally qualified to prosecute and/or defend a person in court. 3. Strictly speaking all ___ are lawyers, but all lawyers are not ___.
bail 1. The main reason for ___ is to ensure a defendant's presence at trial. 2. Sometimes the judge in a criminal case allows an accused defendant to be freed pending trial if the defendant posts ___. 3. Property or money given as a guarantee that a person released from custody will return at a given time is called ___.	**bailiff** 1. A ___ is a minor officer of some courts; the ___ often serves as a messenger or usher. 2. This officer provides security and keeps order in the court. 3. The court reporter, court clerk, and ___ are minor officers of the court.
battery 1. ___ is the unlawful application of force. 2. Even the least touching of another person willfully or in anger is a form of ___. 3. In some jurisdictions, the threat of bodily harm is assault, and if there is actual physical impact, it is ___.	**civil** 1. ___ law comprises the formal rules of a society that deal with personal rights. 2. There are two general types of law: criminal and ___. 3. Torts are ___ wrongs that are recognized by law as grounds for a lawsuit and which can be remedied by awarding damages.

Law Bingo

closing argument 1. It is a speech made at trial after all the evidence has been presented by each party. 2. Unlike an opening statement, a ___ may include opinions. 3. In a ___, the attorney reviews and summarizes the evidence and explains why a certain verdict should be reached.	**contract** 1. A ___ is an agreement between or among parties that is binding under law. 2. One reason someone might sue another is breach of ___. 3. The violation of an agreement that is binding under law is called breach of ___.
court 1. A tribunal presided over by a judge, judges, or a magistrate in civil & criminal cases is called a ___. 2. The ___ reporter records and transcribes a verbatim report of a legal proceeding. 3. To appeal is to ask a higher ___ to reverse the decision of a trial ___.	**crime** 1. A ___ is a violation of a law in which there is injury to the public or a member of the public and for which imprisonment or a fine are possible penalties. 2. A ___ is committed when a person commits a guilty act and has a guilty mind, or *mens rea.* 3. For an act to be a ___ three elements are necessary: a law, a criminal act, and intent.
defendant 1. The ___ is the person accused of violating a criminal or civil law. 2. A summons is a written mandate requiring a ___ to appear in court. 3. A ___ in a criminal trial must plead guilty or not guilty.	**defense** 1. The ___ comprises all the persons, facts, and methods used by a defendant to protect against a prosecutor's or plaintiff's action. 2. Complete this analogy: defend : ___ :: prosecute : prosecution 3. The case presented by or on behalf of the party being accused or sued in a lawsuit is called the ___.
deliberation 1. ___ is a long and careful consideration or discussion. 2. A jury uses ___ to decide upon a verdict. 3. Complete this analogy: ___ : discussion :: intent : purpose	**double jeopardy** 1. ___ forbids a defendant from being tried again on the same charges following a legitimate acquittal or conviction. 2. The ___ clause, found in the 5th Amendment, says one can't be charged with same crime twice. 3. ___ applies to criminal cases only. A civil lawsuit can be brought against a defendant convicted of a crime for damages.
due process 1. ___ is the guarantee that all legal proceedings will be fair and timely. 2. The Fifth Amendment says no one shall be "deprived of life, liberty or property without ___ of law." 3. The Fourteenth Amendment says that states are also obliged to assure ___ of law.	**evidence** 1. ___ refers to any matter of fact that a party in a legal proceeding offers to prove or disprove an issue in the case. 2. There are two basic types of ___: testimonial and physical. 3. Physical, or real, ___ comprises tangible items such as hairs, fibers, latent fingerprints, and biological material.

Law Bingo

examination 1. Direct ___ is the initial questioning of a witness by the side that called him or her. 2. Cross-___ is the act of asking a series of questions designed to verify or discredit answers to questions previously asked. 3. In a trial, ___ is the the interrogation of a witness to elicit his or her testimony.	**felony (-ies)** 1. ___ are offenses that may result in prison sentences of more than one year. Murder, arson, and kidnapping are all ___. 2. Criminal acts fall into two main categories: ___ and misdemeanors. 3. The primary difference between ___ and misdemeanors is the amount of jail time that a convicted offender can be sentenced to serve.
forensic 1. The adjective ___ comes from the Latin word *forensis,* meaning "in open court" or "public." 2. Evidence that can be used in a court that is based on science is called ___ evidence. 3. Blood tests, ballistics, and DNA are types of ___ evidence.	**fraud** 1. ___ involves the intentional misrepresentation or concealment of an important fact upon which the victim is meant to rely. 2. In ___ the victim relies on a concealed or misrepresented fact and is harmed in some way. 3. ___ is the intentional use of some dishonest means to deprive another of money, property, or a legal right.
guilty 1. If one is willing to accept legal responsibility for a criminal act, he or she pleads ___. 2. If a jury finds that a defendant has committed a crime, it returns a verdict of ___. 3. A verdict of "not ___," indicates the jury's conclusion that the prosecution did not meet its burden of proof; it does not mean the defendant is innocent.	**homicide(s)** 1. ___ include all killings of humans; not all ___ are crimes. 2. Murder and manslaughter are ___ that are crimes. 3. A killing committed in justified self-defense is a ___, but it is not a crime.
incarceration (incarcerated) 1. ___ is the confinement in a jail, prison, or penitentiary. 2. People awaiting trial or serving short sentences are usually ___ in jails. 3. People convicted of serious crimes are ___ in prisons and penitentiaries. Those convicted of less serious crimes are often ___ in jails.	**indictment** 1. If a grand jury decides that the evidence presented establishes probable cause, it issues an ___ against the accused. 2. An ___ is the action of formally accusing a person of an offense. 3. Complete this analogy: indict : ___ :: sue : suit
judge(s) 1. A ___ is a public official authorized to decide questions brought before a court of law. 2. The bench is where a ___ sits in court. The term sometimes refers to the ___ him- or herself. 3. In a trial, the ___ decides what evidence is admissible and instructs the jury on how to apply the law based upon the facts presented.	**judicial** 1. The term ___ means "pertaining to the administration of justice, the courts, or a judge." 2. The branch of government that includes courts of law and judges is the ___ branch. 3. Complete this analogy: Supreme Court : Judicial :: Congress : Legislative

Law Bingo

jury 1. A ___ is a body of people sworn to give a verdict in a legal case on the basis of evidence submitted to them in court. 2. People on a ___ are called jurors. The chair and spokesperson for a ___ is its foreperson. 3. In some cases, a grand ___ is selected to examine the validity of an accusation before trial.	**law** 1. A ___ is a rule that if broken subjects a party to criminal punishment or civil liability. 2. Jurisprudence is the study of ___. 3. A statute is written ___ passed by a legislative body.
liability (liable) 1. ___ means legal responsibility for one's acts or omissions. 2. To be legally answerable for something is to be ___. 3. You are ___ for damage caused by your action.	**malice** 1. ___ refers to a party's intention to do injury to another party. 2. It is the intentional unjustified commission of a wrongful act with the intent to cause harm. 3. The conscious violation of the law that injures another individual is called ___.
Miranda rule 1. The ___ states that officer of the law must warn a person taken into custody of the right to remain silent and to legal counsel. 2. This ruling is based upon a U.S. Supreme Court decision in a 1966 case. 3. The ___ requires that a criminal suspect be told of his or her constitutional rights before being interrogated.	**misdemeanor(s)** 1. Criminal acts fall into two categories: felonies and ___ 2. ___ carry sentences of one year or less. 3. Speeding and driving without a license are classified as ___.
motive 1. ___ is the term used to explain why a person committed a crime. 2. Although prosecutors often use ___ to try to convince the jury of the defendant's guilt, ___ is not a criminal element. 3. ___ is sometimes used to explain why a person acted or refused to act in a certain way.	**murder** 1. An intentional, unlawful homicide committed with intent to harm or kill or with reckless disregard for life is ___. 2. In some states the crime of ___ is a capital offense, meaning it is punishable by death. 3. When the killing is deliberate and premeditated, the crime is first-degree ___.
objection 1. An ___ is a formal protest raised in court. 2. If the judge thinks testimony or evidence in question would be a violation, then the ___ would be sustained. 3. If the judge thinks testimony or evidence in question not would be a violation, then the ___ would be overruled.	**plaintiff** 1. A ___ is someone who brings a lawsuit against someone into court. 2. A synonym for ___ is "complainant." 3. In a lawsuit, the ___ is the complaining party; the defendant attempts to protect himself from allegations.

Law Bingo

plea 1. At the arraignment the defendant enters a ___ of guilty or not guilty. 2. It is the formal response by a defendant. 3. If a defendant pleads not guilty, a trial takes place unless a ___ agreement can be reached.	**prosecution** 1. In criminal law, the attorney who charges and tries the case against a person accused of a crime is referred to as the ___. 2. In a criminal trial, the ___ has the burden of proof and must prove its case beyond a reasonable doubt. 3. The government's side in a criminal case is called the ___.
reasonable doubt 1. In a criminal trial, the prosecution has the burden of proof and must prove its case beyond a ___. 2. If a defendant has not been proven guilty beyond a ___, the jury must vote for an acquittal. 3. Evidence that is beyond ___ is the standard required for a criminal conviction.	**sentence** 1. A ___ is the punishment given to a person found guilty of a crime. 2. A synonym for ___ is "punishment." 3. To ___ is to assign punishment to a defendant found guilty by a court.
testimony 1. A formal written or spoken statement given in a court of law is called ___. 2. Perjury is the offense of willfully giving false ___ in court. 3. When you give ___, you tell what you saw, heard, or know.	**theft** 1. The fraudulent taking of another person's personal property with the intent to permanently deprive them of it is ___. A synonym is *larceny*. 2. Burglary is entry into a building illegally with intent to commit a crime, especially ___. 3. Grand ___ occurs when property is stolen that is worth more than the limit for petty ___.
trial 1. It is a legal procedure through which a person's innocence, guilt, or liability is to be determined. 2.Complete this analogy: ___ : try :: arraignment : arraign 3. A "hung jury" results in a mis___.	**verdict** 1. The formal decision made by a jury regarding the questions submitted to it during a trial is the ___. 2. The judge must accept the juiry's decision, or ___, for it to be final. 3. In a criminal case, the jury may reach a ___ of guilty or not guilty.
warrant 1. A ___ is a written order issued by a judicial officer permitting an act that otherwise violates individual rights. 2. There are 3 types of criminal ___: arrest ___, search___, and bench ___. 3. A search ___ permits a law enforcement officer to search a specific place and/or person.	**witness** 1. A person who gives testimony under oath in a court of law is a ___ 2. If you know something about a crime, you might be subpoenaed to serve as a ___. 3. If a ___ does not tell the truth in a court of law, he or she is guilty of perjury.

Law Bingo

© Barbara M Peller

Law
Bingo

murder	acquit (acquittal)	allegation	examination	arraignment
due process	alibi	verdict	jury	testimony
trial	judicial		Miranda rule	warrant
theft	plea	sentence	judge(s)	liability (liable)
malice	fraud	defense	prosecution	battery

Law Bingo

theft	trial	homicide(s)	objection	indictment
liability (liable)	deliberation	bailiff	plea	contract
closing argument	fraud		guilty	sentence
misdemeanor(s)	motive	judicial	witness	arraignment
testimony	verdict	defense	due process	prosecution

Law Bingo: Card No. 2

Law
Bingo

fraud	sentence	deliberation	judge(s)	trial
liability (liable)	alibi	civil	acquit (acquittal)	forensic
plea	verdict		contract	appeal
judicial	closing argument	malice	indictment	homicide(s)
prosecution	court	defense	witness	misdemeanor(s)

Law
Bingo

judicial	contract	allegation	court	indictment
law	bail	acquit (acquittal)	objection	trial
Miranda rule	misdemeanor(s)		battery	examination
sentence	alibi	verdict	defense	bailiff
crime	testimony	attorney-at-law (attorneys)	prosecution	warrant

Law
Bingo

testimony	arraignment	plea	bailiff	court
law	sentence	civil	guilty	alibi
allegation	warrant		jury	felony (-ies)
battery	misdemeanor(s)	murder	witness	defendant
deliberation	defense	trial	judicial	Miranda rule

Law
Bingo

appeal	contract	homicide(s)	misdemeanor(s)	warrant
judge(s)	plea	defendant	acquit (acquittal)	trial
objection	crime		bail	guilty
defense	malice	witness	attorney-at-law (attorneys)	allegation
liability (liable)	bailiff	murder	Miranda rule	double jeopardy

Law
Bingo

murder	contract	felony (-ies)	sentence	deliberation
liability (liable)	indictment	fraud	alibi	law
warrant	examination		guilty	bail
judicial	misdemeanor(s)	civil	theft	closing argument
defense	court	witness	attorney-at-law (attorneys)	appeal

Law
Bingo

Miranda rule	contract	evidence	judge(s)	bail
law	allegation	objection	warrant	bailiff
double jeopardy	court		indictment	arraignment
prosecution	judicial	theft	crime	misdemeanor(s)
verdict	defense	attorney-at-law (attorneys)	plea	liability (liable)

Law Bingo

guilty	deliberation	fraud	double jeopardy	court
crime	indictment	Miranda rule	plea	contract
forensic	murder		alibi	evidence
defendant	arraignment	malice	jury	felony (-ies)
misdemeanor(s)	witness	civil	theft	battery

Law
Bingo

theft	judge(s)	bail	objection	double jeopardy
warrant	bailiff	acquit acquittal)	alibi	misdemeanor(s)
court	contract		examination	closing argument
malice	battery	defendant	witness	forensic
civil	liability (liable)	homicide(s)	testimony	Miranda rule

Law Bingo

appeal	contract	plea	defendant	liability (liable)
evidence	forensic	jury	guilty	acquit (acquittal)
law	misdemeanor(s)		homicide(s)	fraud
civil	trial	witness	court	theft
crime	defense	murder	attorney-at-law (attorneys)	deliberation

Law
Bingo

deliberation	arraignment	forensic	judge(s)	guilty
fraud	liability (liable)	allegation	attorney-at-law (attorneys)	alibi
murder	felony (-ies)		warrant	objection
defense	indictment	misdemeanor(s)	theft	law
contract	evidence	court	crime	bailiff

Law
Bingo

defendant	arraignment	appeal	forensic	warrant
allegation	evidence	misdemeanor(s)	guilty	closing argument
judge(s)	bailiff		fraud	felony (-ies)
Miranda rule	witness	bail	court	theft
defense	battery	attorney-at-law (attorneys)	murder	jury

Law
Bingo

due process	misdemeanor(s)	plea	guilty	crime
bailiff	murder	forensic	alibi	contract
defendant	examination		homicide(s)	civil
battery	witness	court	bail	appeal
defense	objection	closing argument	liability (liable)	Miranda rule

Law Bingo

jury	guilty	plea	deliberation	judge(s)
appeal	homicide(s)	acquit (acquittal)	allegation	crime
warrant	murder		trial	contract
defense	forensic	evidence	witness	defendant
liability (liable)	misdemeanor(s)	attorney-at-law (attorneys)	double jeopardy	fraud

Law Bingo

bail	forensic	evidence	double jeopardy	motive
objection	closing argument	felony (-ies)	law	examination
defendant	arraignment		warrant	fraud
judicial	bailiff	defense	jury	theft
crime	reasonable doubt	attorney-at-law (attorneys)	indictment	contract

Law Bingo

civil	plaintiff	incarceration (incarcerated)	forensic	due process
jury	crime	witness	examination	felony (-ies)
guilty	Miranda rule		reasonable doubt	evidence
battery	llability (liable)	theft	plea	closing argument
malice	defendant	deliberation	judge(s)	arraignment

Law Bingo: Card No. 17

Law Bingo

double jeopardy	court	bailiff	defendant	objection
contract	civil	malice	warrant	crime
guilty	closing argument		incarceration (incarcerated)	allegation
arraignment	acquit acquittal)	witness	theft	homicide(s)
reasonable doubt	forensic	plea	plaintiff	appeal

Law Bingo

warrant	appeal	forensic	evidence	theft
jury	judge(s)	contract	deliberation	examination
plaintiff	court		alibi	trial
homicide(s)	reasonable doubt	malice	indictment	incarceration (incarcerated)
allegation	motive	liability (liable)	Miranda rule	attorney-at-law (attorneys)

Law Bingo

due process	plaintiff	judge(s)	forensic	attorney-at-law (attorneys)
bailiff	fraud	law	malice	objection
arraignment	felony (-ies)		judicial	acquit (acquittal)
testimony	verdict	prosecution	indictment	reasonable doubt
sentence	Miranda rule	motive	theft	incarceration (incarcerated)

Law Bingo: Card No. 20

Law Bingo

jury	appeal	law	forensic	testimony
arraignment	incarceration (incarcerated)	bail	evidence	murder
closing argument	liability (liable)		plaintiff	plea
malice	deliberation	reasonable doubt	battery	Miranda rule
judicial	motive	attorney-at-law (attorneys)	civil	indictment

Law Bingo: Card No. 21

Law Bingo

double jeopardy	homicide(s)	incarceration (incarcerated)	allegation	defendant
objection	judge(s)	trial	evidence	alibi
bailiff	examination		murder	felony (-ies)
reasonable doubt	battery	indictment	acquit (acquittal)	law
motive	civil	plaintiff	closing argument	judicial

Law Bingo

bail	plaintiff	deliberation	allegation	attorney-at-law (attorneys)
appeal	due process	liability (liable)	jury	acquit acquittal)
homicide(s)	defendant		prosecution	murder
closing argument	motive	reasonable doubt	civil	indictment
testimony	verdict	Miranda rule	malice	incarceration (incarcerated)

Law Bingo: Card No. 23

Law Bingo

bail	Miranda rule	due process	plaintiff	evidence
incarceration (incarcerated)	attorney-at-law (attorneys)	law	objection	murder
felony (-ies)	double jeopardy		defendant	closing argument
testimony	prosecution	reasonable doubt	civil	arraignment
sentence	judicial	motive	judge(s)	verdict

Law Bingo

judicial	law	plaintiff	plea	incarceration (incarcerated)
acquit (acquittal)	arraignment	jury	bail	alibi
battery	evidence		prosecution	reasonable doubt
trial	testimony	verdict	motive	examination
attorney-at-law (attorneys)	due process	bailiff	crime	sentence

Law Bingo: Card No. 25

Law Bingo

incarceration (incarcerated)	plaintiff	homicide(s)	objection	double jeopardy
malice	judge(s)	evidence	due process	bail
battery	prosecution		examination	judicial
civil	allegation	testimony	motive	reasonable doubt
felony (-ies)	crime	plea	verdict	sentence

Law Bingo

homicide(s)	bailiff	plaintiff	due process	fraud
testimony	prosecution	jury	reasonable doubt	alibi
witness	verdict		motive	judicial
double jeopardy	appeal	law	sentence	acquit (acquittal)
crime	examination	incarceration (incarcerated)	trial	felony (-ies)

Law
Bingo

homicide(s)	due process	trial	plaintiff	bail
fraud	incarceration (incarcerated)	prosecution	objection	examination
verdict	closing argument		felony (-ies)	malice
theft	double jeopardy	liability (liable)	motive	reasonable doubt
allegation	guilty	crime	sentence	testimony

Law
Bingo

incarceration (incarcerated)	due process	double jeopardy	jury	guilty
indictment	malice	law	felony (-ies)	trial
battery	prosecution		alibi	plaintiff
fraud	testimony	indictment	motive	reasonable doubt
bail	evidence	sentence	appeal	verdict

Law
Bingo

court	plaintiff	objection	guilty	reasonable doubt
acquit (acquittal)	due process	homicide(s)	examination	alibi
battery	defendant		felony (-ies)	law
sentence	appeal	allegation	motive	prosecution
testimony	warrant	verdict	incarceration (incarcerated)	trial